101 MOJITOS

and Other Muddled Drinks

Photography © 2011 by Alexandra Grablewski

Food styling by Brian Preston-Campbell

Prop styling by Lynda White

Published by John Wiley & Sons, Inc., Hoboken, New Jersey

Published simultaneously in Canada

For general information about our other products and services, please contact our Customer Care Department within the United States at (800) 762-2974, outside the United States at (317) 572-3993 or fax (317) 572-4002.

Wiley also publishes its books in a variety of electronic formats. Some content that appears in print may not be available in electronic books. For more information about Wiley products, visit our web site at www.wiley.com.

Library of Congress Cataloging-in-Publication Data:

Haasarud, Kim.
  101 mojitos and other muddled drinks / Kim Haasarud ; photography by Alexandra Grablewski.
      p. cm.
  Includes index.
  ISBN 978-0-470-50521-2 (cloth)
  1. Mojitos. 2. Cocktails. I. Title. II. Title: One hundred and one mojitos and other muddled drinks.
  TX951.H2123 2010
  641.8'74--dc22
                              2010011102

Printed in China

10 9 8 7 6 5 4 3 2 1

MOJITOS

and Other Muddled Drinks

KIM HAASARUD

PHOTOGRAPHY BY ALEXANDRA GRABLEWSKI

WILEY

JOHN WILEY & SONS, INC.

Introduction

In the past decade the Mojito has become a staple in many bars across the country. It's refreshing, pretty to look at, and delicious. It has its roots in Cuba and was a favorite of Ernest Hemingway in the 1930s. It is believed to have evolved from a sixteenth-century drink called el Draque (meaning "the dragon"). El draque was created by the English pirate, Richard Drake, who used aguardiente (a primitive relative of rum—barely drinkable by today's standards), sugar, lime, and mint. Others believe that the African slaves who worked in the Cuban sugarcane fields first created the drink. The drink has since evolved to use many kinds of premium rums, different types of sugar, varieties of mint, and so forth.

The Mojito is a very simple drink to make, yet everyone has probably had a bad one. Too sweet, too sour, too strong—I think most people feel the need to doctor it up and put their own spin on it, which is fine if you understand the importance of the basic ingredients, like fresh-squeezed lime juice, and the proper ratios. Below, I'm going to break down the Mojito into its essential components, which include the ingredients, ice, and muddling techniques that will be used in the recipes throughout this book.

INGREDIENTS

2 ounces **rum**

10 to 15 **mint leaves**

1 ounce fresh **lime juice**

1 ounce **simple syrup** (see page 7)

Splash of **soda water**

TOOLS

Muddler

Lime or citrus **squeezer**

THE RUM

There are many varieties of rum, depending on, among other things: what it's distilled from (sugarcane juice or molasses); how it's distilled and extracted; how long it's aged and what it's aged in; where it is grown; and if it is flavored. Subsequently, rum makes for one of the largest spirit categories. For a Mojito, I would recommend a rum on the lighter end of the spectrum, such as Bacardi, Cruzan, or 10 Cane rum. You could use a darker or an aged rum, but I have found that the citrus and mint work best with the lighter ones. Some of the flavored rums, such as Bacardi Limón or Cruzan Guava, also add a nice spin on the

Mojito. (Keep in mind, I'm just speaking about the Mojito; there are many great aged rums mentioned in this book to use with other types of muddled drinks, of which the Mojito is just one.)

FRESH IS BEST

One of the most important elements in a Mojito is fresh-squeezed lime juice. I cannot stress enough the importance of fresh-squeezed versus bottled or a premix off the shelf. It really makes a world of difference. Don't skimp!

Limes can be expensive depending on the time of year and where you buy them, but if you live close to a produce market or visit the farmer's market, you can usually find them much cheaper than at the grocery store. Choose limes that are thin-skinned and somewhat malleable. Those are the ripest and will yield the most juice.

I would encourage you to buy other seasonal ingredients to experiment with. Throughout the book, I give lots of flavor combinations that use a wide range of ingredients, from watermelon to Concord grapes to various fresh herbs. If you see some seasonal ingredients that look good and ripe, by all means, pick them up!

SUGAR

Sugar is an essential ingredient to the Mojito—actually for most muddled cocktails, particularly those that use fresh lemons or limes. Sugar can come in many forms—white sugar, brown sugar, Demerara sugar, syrups, honeys, agave nectar, and so on. I would encourage you to experiment using different sweeteners, for they add other layers of flavor and richness to a drink. Throughout the book, though, I primarily use simple syrup—an equal ratio of sugar to water. All of the syrups that follow are easy to make and can be kept in the fridge for about a week or so.

■ **TIP:** If you are throwing a party, a one liter bottle of rum makes about sixteen Mojitos.

■ **TIP:** One lime will yield approximately one ounce of juice. So, depending on the number of Mojitos you are planning to make, buy the same amount of limes plus a few extra. (Example: 10 Mojitos = about 10 limes.)

Simple Syrup

Makes enough for about 10 Mojitos

2 cups **sugar**

2 cups **water**

In a medium saucepan over medium heat, combine the sugar and water and stir until the sugar is completely dissolved. Let cool completely, then bottle and keep refrigerated until ready to use.

Fresh Berry Syrup

Makes enough for about 10 muddled drinks

2 cups **sugar**

2 cups of **water**

½ cup of **fresh berries** (if using strawberries, hull and cut in half or in quarters)

In a medium saucepan over medium heat, combine the sugar, water, and berries and stir until both the sugar has dissolved and the berries start to bleed into the syrup. Bring to a simmer, then remove from the heat. Let cool completely. Strain, then bottle and keep refrigerated until ready to use.

Lavender Syrup

Makes enough for about 10 muddled drinks

This is used in the Blueberry-Lavender Mojito (see page 31), but can be used in other drinks as well. Do not use potpourri lavender. It is sometimes coated in unedible oils.

2 cups **sugar**

2 cups **water**

1 tablespoon dried **lavender**

In a medium saucepan over medium heat, combine the sugar, water, and lavender. Stir until the sugar has dissolved. Bring to a simmer, then remove from the heat. Let cool completely. Strain, then bottle and keep refrigerated until ready to use.

Honey Water

Makes enough for about 10 muddled drinks

A great alternative to simple syrup.

2 cups **honey** (any type will do)

2 cups **water**

In a medium saucepan over medium heat, combine the honey and water and stir until completely combined. Let cool completely, then bottle and keep refrigerated until ready to use.

There are some reputable companies that sell great syrups, agave nectars, and other sweeteners, such as Monin, who carries nearly 100 syrups and nectars. They can be ordered online at Monin.com, and they'll ship directly to your home or business.

THE MINT

You really need a good amount of mint to make a Mojito, about 10 to 15 leaves. If possible, use the smaller leaves; the big "elephant ear" leaves are usually a little bitter and sometimes devoid of flavor. Also, there are many kinds of mint available at farmer's markets, ranging from pineapple to lemon to chocolate mint. One Wednesday at the Santa Monica farmer's market, I actually found some "Bob Marley Mint" seedlings and planted them in my garden. Supposedly, it was a hybrid mint that had grown on Bob Marley's stoop in Jamaica. Or at least I think it was mint . . . hmmmm . . . it did have some subtle smokiness to it. Anyway, the point being, mint seedlings are easy to find at farmer's markets, they grow rapidly, and are easy to maintain, even if you just have a small pot on your windowsill. Nothing beats having fresh mint right in your own home. If you've never planted mint before, be warned: it can overtake other plants in your garden. So, I usually grow mint in a separate planter.

THE ICE

In making a Mojito, I find that crushed ice works the best for several reasons: 1) it acts as a sieve between the muddled components and your mouth, so that you don't get a mouth full of crushed mint or fruit pulp when taking a sip; 2) it chills the drink very, very fast. Since this is a drink usually served in the warm, hot months, a cold drink is a better drink; and 3) it dilutes the drink faster. That may sound like something you would not want

to happen, but in a Mojito, you need that water. In fact, the longer it sits out and dilutes, the better it gets. A Mojito made with crushed ice can literally sit on a countertop for about 20 minutes and be just as good a drink as when you first made it, maybe even better.

MUDDLING

Muddling is not a four-letter word, contrary to what some bartenders may tell you. The truth is, many bartenders do not muddle correctly and overdo it, making more work for themselves than necessary. I love my muddler. Truth be told, if I were stranded on a desert island and could only have one bar tool, it would be my muddler. (Okay, I'd probably use it for protection against wild beasts, but that's beside the point.) I find that muddled drinks make the best cocktails. Why muddle when you can just buy fresh juice or purees, you might ask? Ahhhh, well, when muddling a lemon or orange wedge, for example, you are not only extracting fresh juice from the fruit, but also extracting some essential oils from the skin, which make for a much more flavorful and aromatic cocktail. It's also the easiest way to pulverize cucumber or fresh berries or melon, and it is the perfect ice crusher. You can use it to muddle almost any fruit, but there are some varying techniques you should be aware of, which I cover below. David Nepove (aka "Mister Mojito") sells a variety of muddlers on his web site—www.mistermojito.com—that I highly recommend. I was recently talking to someone who said they always use a mortar and pestle for muddled drinks; to each his own, but I fear for your knuckles and the splatter cleanup if you choose to go that route.

THE "PRESS" *(Muddling Herbs)*

I can't tell you how many times I witness bartenders going to town with a muddler, pulverizing the heck out of some mint. NOT NECESSARY. With herbs—such as mint, sage, basil—you really just want to press them to extract the essential oils; that's it! The goal is not to pulverize the herbs into a gazillion little pieces, but to merely bruise them. (In fact, try putting a few mint leaves in your mouth and pulverize them with your teeth—pretty bitter.)

How to Do It: Place the herbs in the bottom of a cocktail glass. Add any sweetener or other juice you may be using. Be sure the widest end of the muddler—the end with the most surface area—is the end that will be touching the herbs. With one hand holding the glass, use the other to muddle the herbs lightly. Five or six presses is all it takes—and voilà!

THE "CITRUS CRUSH" *(Muddling Citrus Fruits)*

The goal behind muddling (or crushing) citrus fruits (such as oranges, lemons, limes, and grapefruits) is twofold: 1) to extract the juice from the fruit; and 2) to extract some essential oils from the skin.

How to Do It: The first step is to cut the citrus fruits into nice wedges or chunks to make them easy to work with and to get the most flavor out of them. The second step is to place the wedges into the cocktail glass and add the sweetener and any other juices you plan on using. The third step is to place the widest end of the muddler inside the glass and press down, hard. This may take some umph to really extract the juice out of the fruit, maybe 6 to 10 presses.

Note: In some cases, you may be muddling citrus fruits with herbs. Always place the herbs in first, then any citrus fruits on top. Once you start crushing the fruit, the fruit will bruise the herbs. Also, be careful to not pulverize the citrus fruit. Pulverizing it (breaking it into smaller pieces) will expose the white pith in the peel, which is pretty bitter.

THE "PULVERIZER" *(Muddling All Other Fruits and Vegetables)*

The goal behind muddling (or pulverizing) fruits and vegetables is to pulp them, or make them it into a chunky puree.

How to Do It: Simply place the fruit or vegetables into the bottom of a cocktail glass along with any sweetener or juice you may be using. Using the widest end of the muddler, muddle the contents until the fruit is pulped.

THE "SEATTLE MUDDLE" *(Muddling with Ice)*

I'm not sure who started this one, but apparently bartenders in Seattle throw in some ice when muddling. They say it helps to crush the fruit better. I don't recommend using ice when muddling if you're just trying to bruise some herbs. (It pulverizes them—not a good thing.) But, I have found a cube of ice helpful when trying to pulverize fruits or vegetables with tougher skin or harder flesh, such as cucumbers or apples.

How to Do It: The method is the same as the Pulverizer, but add a cube or two of ice.

THE RATIOS

One of the most important factors in making a Mojito (besides using fresh-squeezed lime juice) is understanding the ratio of lime juice to simple syrup. It's a simple 1:1 ratio. Use a jigger. I've been working in this industry for over 20 years and I still use a jigger, because if you're off even ¼ of an ounce, you just threw off the entire drink. You get the ratio right, and you're good to go.

Mojito Party

So, now that you have all the tools and ingredients ready, here's how to make the perfect Mojito, step-by-step. If I'm having guests over, I prep all my ingredients in advance so that I can make everything fairly quickly, or better yet, people can make one for themselves!

PREP

Step 1: Prepping the Mint. Pluck all the mint leaves from the stems and place in a bowl. (Put a moist paper towel over the leaves to prevent them from wilting.)

Step 2: Prepping the Lime Juice. Have a small pitcher or carafe handy to hold your lime juice. Wash the limes thoroughly. (Many farmers seal their citrus fruits with wax—that's why they always look so shiny!) Cut the nubs off each end of the lime, then cut in half width-wise. Place one half in a lime squeezer, pulp side down, and give it a good press to extract the juice into your small carafe or pitcher. It is up to you to strain your lime juice. If you are juicing over two dozen limes, I would opt to strain it. If you don't, the pulp will float to the top and the first few drinks you make will be pretty pulpy.

Step 3: Prep the Simple Syrup. Make the simple syrup (see page 7) and keep it in a small carafe or pitcher.

Step 4: Prep the Other Fruits. If using any other fruits, wash and cut them into chunks, if applicable. Place in a nice bowl. If you are including apples or pears, squeeze some lemon on top of them to prevent browning.

Step 5: Other Items to Have on the Mojito Table. The rum, muddler(s), jigger, glassware, big bowl of crushed ice, soda water, and stirrers.

MAKING THE MOJITOS

Now that all the prep work is done, making the mojitos is simple:

Step 1: In the rocks glass, muddle 10–15 mint leaves with 1 ounce lime juice, 1 ounce simple syrup (and any other fresh fruit you might be using).

Step 2: Add 2 ounces rum.

Step 3: Top with crushed ice.

Step 4: Top with a splash of soda water and stir well! Garnish with a mint sprig (or piece of fresh fruit) and serve!

HAPPY MUDDLING!

The Perfect MOJITO

See the Introduction for a complete analysis of the Mojito, from muddling techniques, to type of ice, rum, and so forth. This is a very simple and delicious drink to make, but unfortunately it gets muddled up (literally) too often. There are two important keys that will guarantee a perfect Mojito every time. First, you must use fresh-squeezed lime juice. No premixes or bottled lime juice here—they just won't cut it. Second,the lime juice to simple syrup ratio must be 1:1. Do not take liberties. Use a jigger for accuracy. If you get those two things right, you'll be making perfect Mojitos at every party!

10 to 15 **mint leaves**, plus sprig for garnish

1 ounce fresh **lime juice**

1 ounce **simple syrup** (see page 7)

2 ounces premium **rum** (such as 10 Cane, Bacardi Superior, Cruzan, etc.)

Splash of **soda water**

In the bottom of a rocks glass, muddle the mint leaves with the lime juice and simple syrup. (Muddle lightly to just release the oils in the mint, do not pulverize the leaves.) Add the rum. Top with crushed ice and the soda water. Stir well from the bottom up. Garnish with the mint sprig and serve.

Brut MOJITO

Same recipe as above, except muddle the mint, lime juice, and simple syrup in a mixing glass, add the rum, shake it with ice. Pour into a tall glass and top with a dash of bitters and a splash of champagne. Add additional ice, if needed.

3/4

Grand MOJITO

An upscale version using Grand Marnier and mud-dled fresh oranges.

- 5 **mint leaves**, plus sprig for garnish
- 2 **orange wedges**, plus 1 half-wheel for garnish
- 1 ounce fresh **lime juice**
- 1 ounce **simple syrup** (see page 7)
- 1½ ounces **light rum**
- ½ ounce **Grand Marnier**
- Splash of **soda water**

In a tall glass, muddle the mint leaves with the orange wedges, lime juice, and simple syrup. Add the rum and Grand Marnier. Top with crushed ice and the soda water. Stir well from the bottom up. Garnish with the mint sprig and orange half-wheel.

Grand Mango MOJITO

Same recipe as above but add ¼ cup fresh mango chunks or use mango syrup in lieu of the simple syrup.

5

Black & Blue Mojito

10 **mint leaves**, plus sprig for garnish

1 ounce fresh **lime juice**

1 ounce **blueberry** or **blackberry syrup** (see page 7)
or blueberry or blackberry pie filling

10 ripe **blueberries** or 5 **blackberries**, plus extra for garnish

2 ounces **light rum**

Splash of **soda water**

In a rocks or highball glass, muddle the mint leaves with the lime
juice, syrup, and blueberries or blackberries. Be sure the berries are fully pulped. Add the rum. Top with crushed ice and the
soda water. Stir well from the bottom up. Garnish with the mint
sprig and remaining berries.

6

Sparkling Raspberry
Mojito

I created this cocktail for Wyndham Worldwide hotels and resorts. We wanted a variation of the Mojito that was more seasonal, fruity, and colorful.

10 **mint leaves**, plus sprig for garnish

6 ripe **raspberries**, plus extra for garnish

1 ounce fresh **lime juice**

1 ounce **simple syrup** (see page 7) or **raspberry syrup** (for more raspberry flavor, if desired)

1½ ounces **light rum**

½ ounce **raspberry liqueur** (optional)

Splash of **rosé champagne** (such as Chandon Rosé)

In a highball glass, muddle the mint leaves with 6 of the raspberries, the lime juice, and simple syrup. Add the rum and raspberry liqueur, if desired. Top with crushed ice and rosé. Stir well from the bottom up. Garnish with the mint sprig and remaining raspberries.

7

Mandarin & Mango MOJITO

Created by Philip Raimondo, Master Mixologist for
Beam Global Spirits & Wine.

8 to 10 **mint leaves**, plus sprig for garnish

5 Mandarin **orange wedges**, plus 1 for garnish (jarred or canned
can be substituted when fresh are unavailable)

½ ounce fresh **orange juice**

1½ ounces Cruzan Mango **rum**

1 ounce fresh **lime juice**

1 ounce **simple syrup** (see page 7) or **agave nectar**

½ ounce DeKuyper **Orange Curaçao** or **triple sec**

Splash of **soda water** or **7-Up**

Lime wedge, for garnish

In a mixing glass, add the mint leaves, 5 of the orange wedges,
and the orange juice. Lightly muddle the oranges into the mint
leaves. Add the rum, lime juice, simple syrup, and curaçao and fill
the glass with ice. Give it a quick shake and transfer to a serving
glass. Add more ice if needed, then top with the soda water.
Garnish with the lime wedge, mint sprig, and remaining orange
wedge.

8

Napa Valley MOJITO

A taste of Napa all the way through.

10 **mint leaves**

10 red and white seedless **grapes**, plus extra for garnish

1 ounce fresh **lime juice**

1 ounce **simple syrup** (see page 7)

1½ ounces **rum**

Splash of **sparkling wine** (such as Chandon Brut from the Napa Valley or Nectar Imperial, which is sweeter)

In a tall glass, muddle the mint leaves with 10 of the grapes, lime juice, and simple syrup. Add the rum. Top with crushed ice and sparkling wine. Stir well from the bottom up. Garnish with the remaining grapes.

Cucumber-Cilantro MOJITO

From my friend, Debbi Peek, a mixologist from Chicago, Illinois.

2 slices hothouse **cucumber**

10 to 12 **cilantro leaves**, plus sprig for garnish

1 ounce fresh **lime juice**

1 ounce **simple syrup** (see page 7)

1½ ounces Bacardi Limón **rum**

Splash of **7-Up**

Lime wedge, for garnish

In a tall glass, muddle the cucumber, cilantro leaves, lime juice, and simple syrup. Add ice and the rum. Top with 7-Up. Stir from the bottom up. Garnish with the sprig of cilantro and lime wedge.

Blackberry-Pom MOJITO

5 to 7 **mint leaves**, plus sprig for garnish

3 ripe **blackberries**, plus 1 for garnish

1 ounce fresh **lime juice**

1 ounce **blackberry syrup** or **simple syrup** (see page 7)

Splash of **pomegranate juice**

2 ounces **light rum**

Splash of **soda water**

In a tall glass, muddle the mint leaves with 3 of the blackberries, lime juice, blackberry syrup, and pomegranate juice. Add the rum. Top with crushed ice and the soda water. Stir well from the bottom up. Garnish with the remaining blackberries and mint sprig.

11

Pineapple-Ginger MOJITO

Perry's Steakhouse in Texas sells these by the dozen!
Very good with grilled meats and barbecue.

¼ cup fresh **pineapple chunks**

10 **mint leaves**

1 ounce fresh **lime juice**

1 ounce **simple syrup** (see page 7)

1½ ounces 10 Cane **rum**

½ ounce Domaine de Canton **ginger liqueur**

1 ounce **ginger beer** or **ginger ale**

Pineapple wedge or leaf and candied ginger (optional), for garnish

In a tall glass, muddle the pineapple chunks with the mint leaves,
lime juice, and simple syrup. Add the rum and ginger liqueur. Top
with crushed ice and ginger beer. Stir well from the bottom up.
Garnish with the pineapple wedge and candied ginger, if desired.

12

Watermelon-Basil MOJITO

This cocktail is only appropriate for the summer months when fresh watermelon is at its peak and the sweetest. You can always pump up the watermelon flavor by adding just a touch of watermelon liqueur, such as Pucker.

⅓ cup fresh **watermelon chunks**

1 ounce fresh **lime juice**

1 ounce **simple syrup** (see page 7)

4 **basil leaves**, plus sprig for garnish

1½ ounces **light rum**

½ ounce **watermelon schnapps** (such as Pucker; optional)

Splash of **soda water**

Watermelon rind, for garnish

In a cocktail glass, muddle the watermelon with the lime juice, simple syrup, and basil leaves. Add the rum and watermelon schnapps, if desired. Top with crushed ice and the soda water. Stir well from the bottom up. Garnish with the basil sprig and watermelon rind and serve.

13

Key West MOJITO

This is a great tart and sweet Mojito—a little more intense on the tart than the sweet—great for those hot summer days. I shake this Mojito to make it smoother and colder.

10 **mint leaves**

¼ cup fresh **pineapple chunks**

1 ounce **Key lime juice** (such as Nelly & Joe's)

1 ounce **simple syrup** (see page 7)

1 ounce **light rum**

½ ounce **Midori**

Splash of **soda water**

Lime wheel and **pineapple leaf**, for garnish

In a mixing glass, muddle the mint leaves with the pineapple chunks, Key lime juice, and simple syrup. Add the rum and Midori. Top with ice and shake vigorously. Pour into a tall glass. Add additional ice, if needed. Top with the soda water and stir. Garnish with the lime wheel and pineapple leaf.

14/15

Blueberry-Lavender
Mojito

From my friend, Bridget Albert, Master Mixologist and author of Market Fresh Mixology.

10 to 15 **mint leaves**

1 ounce **lavender syrup** or **simple syrup** (see page 7)

½ ounce fresh **lime juice**

15 ripe **blueberries**, plus extra for garnish

1½ ounces **light rum**

Splash of **soda water**

In a tall glass, muddle the mint leaves, lavender syrup, lime juice, 10 of the blueberries, and rum. Muddle just enough to combine the flavors, being careful not to over-muddle. Fill a glass with crushed ice. Top with the soda water. Stir with bar spoon until well blended. Garnish with the remaining blueberries.

Passion Fruit–Sage Mojito

3 **sage leaves**, plus 1 for garnish

1 ounce **passion fruit puree**

1 ounce fresh **lime juice**

1 ounce **simple syrup** (see page 7)

1½ ounces **aged rum**

Splash of **Grand Marnier** (optional)

Splash of **soda water**

In a cocktail glass, muddle 3 of the sage leaves with the passion fruit puree, lime juice, and simple syrup. Add the rum and Grand Marnier, if desired. Top with ice and pour into a cocktail shaker. Shake vigorously. Pour back into the cocktail glass. Top with the soda water and stir. Garnish with the remaining sage leaf.

16

White Pear MOJITO

A delicious combination of fresh pear and white grapes. I strain this one because there is quite a bit of pulp, and I like it a little cleaner, but if you like the big chunks of fruit, feel free just to top with the ice and stir it instead.

7 to 10 **mint leaves**, plus sprig for garnish

10 white seedless **grapes**, plus extra for garnish

½ ripe **pear** (Bartletts work best), plus slice for garnish

1 ounce fresh **lime juice**

1 ounce **simple syrup** (see page 7)

2 ounces Bacardi Limón **rum**

Splash of **soda water**

In a mixing glass, muddle the mint leaves with 10 of the grapes, the pear, lime juice, and simple syrup. Add the rum and top with ice. Shake vigorously. Strain into a rocks glass filled with ice. Top with the soda water and stir. Garnish with the pear slice, remaining speared grapes, and mint sprig.

17

San Vincente CRUSH

From Natalie Bovis-Nelsen, The Liquid Muse. Saint Vincent is the patron saint of winemakers, and pisco is the result of an abundance of grapes in Peru and Chile. Conquistadors had brought grapevines with them to make wine for mass. The grapes flourished, so they distilled the excess fermented juice, making the grape-based spirit called pisco.

1 **lemon wedge**

Powdered **sugar**, for garnishing rim

5 red seedless **grapes**

1 heaping tablespoon torn fresh **basil**, plus basil leaf for garnish

2 ounces **pisco**

¾ ounce fresh **lemon juice**

¾ ounce **simple syrup** (see page 7)

Wet the rim of a martini glass with a lemon wedge, then dip it into a small plate of powdered sugar. Set aside. Muddle the grapes and torn basil in the bottom of a mixing glass until the juice from the grapes has been extracted. Add the pisco, lemon juice, and simple syrup. Add ice and shake hard. Strain into the rimmed martini glass. Garnish with the basil leaf.

Pomegranate Ruby MOJITO

10 **mint leaves**, plus sprig for garnish

2 ruby red **grapefruit wedges**

½ ounce fresh **lime juice**

1 ounce **simple syrup** (see page 7)

½ ounce **pomegranate juice** (such as POM Wonderful)

1½ ounces **rum**

Splash of **soda water**

1 teaspoon **pomegranate seeds**

In a cocktail shaker, muddle the mint leaves with the grapefruit wedges, lime juice, simple syrup, and pomegranate juice. Add the rum and top with ice. Shake vigorously. Strain into a tall glass filled with ice. Add the soda water. Garnish with the pomegranate seeds and mint sprig.

Pacific Pear MOJITO

10 **mint leaves**, plus sprig for garnish

¼ cup fresh **pear chunks** (Bartletts work best) or 1 ounce **pear nectar**, plus pear slice, for garnish

1 ounce fresh **lime juice**

1 ounce **simple syrup** (see page 7)

¾ ounce **light rum**

¾ ounce dry **sake**

½ ounce **pear liqueur** (such as Mathilde Poires)

Splash of **soda water**

In a cocktail glass, muddle the mint leaves with the pear chunks, lime juice, and simple syrup. Add the rum, sake, and pear liqueur. Top with crushed ice. Add the soda water. Stir well from the bottom up. Garnish with the mint sprig and pear slice.

20

Stormy Ginger MOJITO

One year I helped cater a private party on a yacht going to Catalina Island and created this drink for the guests. (FYI, ginger is known for helping to combat seasickness.) This is a Mojito variation of the classic Dark and Stormy.

10 **mint leaves**, plus sprig for garnish

4 or 5 slices peeled **fresh ginger**

1 ounce fresh **lime juice**

1 ounce **simple syrup** (see page 7)

1½ ounces **light rum**

Splash of **ginger beer**

Float of Goslings or Cruzan Black Strap **rum** (optional)

Piece of **candied ginger**, for garnish (optional)

In a mixing glass, muddle the mint leaves with the fresh ginger, lime juice, and simple syrup. Add the rum. Top with crushed ice. Add the ginger beer. Stir well from the bottom up. Garnish with the mint sprig and candied ginger, if desired. Add a float of Goslings or Cruzan Black Strap rum, if desired.

21

Blood Orange MOJITO

10 **mint leaves**, plus sprig for garnish

4 **blood orange wedges** or **blood orange puree**
(such as Boiron or Perfect Puree), plus 1 wheel for garnish

1 ounce fresh **lime juice**

1 ounce **simple syrup** (see page 7)

1½ ounces **rum**

Splash of **Grand Marnier** (optional)

Splash of **soda water**

In a cocktail glass, muddle the mint leaves with the orange
wedges, lime juice, and simple syrup. Add the rum and Grand
Marnier, if desired. Top with crushed ice. Top with the soda
water. Stir well from the bottom up. Garnish with the orange
wheel and mint sprig.

22

Pomegranate-Mandarin
MOJITO

10 **mint leaves**, plus sprig for garnish

1 **clementine orange**, peeled and segmented, plus peel for garnish

½ ounce **pomegranate juice**

1 ounce fresh **lime juice**

1 ounce **simple syrup** (see page 7)

1½ ounces **light rum**

½ ounce **triple sec**

Splash of **soda water**

In a cocktail glass, muddle the mint leaves with the orange seg-ments, pomegranate juice, lime juice, and simple syrup. Add the rum and triple sec. Top with crushed ice and the soda water. Stir well from the bottom up. Garnish with the mint sprig and orange peel.

23/24

Caipirinha

A Caipirinha is similar to a Mojito, but made with cachaça, a Brazilian rum, and without the mint. You also muddle the actual lime, instead of using fresh lime juice. It's a wonderfully refreshing drink and can be quite addictive. I would recommend using a higher-end cachaça—like Leblon or Cabana Cachaça—that has a lot of citrus and floral aromas, versus the cheaper stuff, which can burn your nose with just a sniff.

You can also make a Caipiroska by using vodka instead of cachaça. It won't have the same earthy flavor that cachaça adds to the drink, but it's still very good.

4 **lime wedges**

1 ounce **simple syrup** (see page 7)

2 ounces **cachaça**

In a rocks glass, muddle the lime wedges with the simple syrup. Add the cachaça. Top with ice and pour into a cocktail shaker. Shake vigorously and pour back into the rocks glass.

Uva (Grape) CAIPIRINHA

Same recipe as above, but add 10 red and white seedless grapes and muddle with the other ingredients. Also, for a little more grape flavor, use equal parts cachaça and grape flavored vodka such as SKYY or Three Olives.

25

Watermelon-Yuzu
CAIPIRINHA

Yuzu is a Japanese citrus fruit. It tastes like a cross between a grapefruit and a Mandarin orange, but is very tart. Yuzu juice can be found in most specialty grocers or online. I find that it accents and makes sweet watermelon pop with flavor. Also, if desired, you can add a touch of watermelon schnapps for more flavor.

¼ cup fresh **watermelon chunks**, plus wedge, for garnish

1 teaspoon **yuzu juice**

2 **lime wedges**

1 ounce **simple syrup** (see page 7)

2 ounces **cachaça**

½ ounce **watermelon schnapps** (such as Pucker; optional)

In a rocks glass, muddle the watermelon chunks with the yuzu juice, lime wedges, and simple syrup. Add the cachaça and watermelon schnapps, if using. Fill with ice and pour into a cocktail shaker. Shake vigorously and pour back into the rocks glass. Garnish with the watermelon wedge.

Strawberry-Pineapple
CAIPIRINHA

2 ripe **strawberries**, hulled, plus 1 strawberry half for garnish

¼ cup fresh **pineapple chunks**, plus wedge for garnish

4 **lime wedges**

1 ounce **simple syrup** (see page 7)

2 ounces **cachaça**

Fill a rocks glass with ice and set aside. In a mixing glass, muddle 2 of the strawberries with the pineapple chunks, lime wedges, and simple syrup. Add the cachaça and top with ice. Shake vigorously and strain into the iced rocks glass. (Because this drink contains so much pulp and fruit, I like to strain it. But if you like a lot of fruit pulp, pour the shaken contents into the glass.) Garnish with the strawberry half and pineapple wedge.

Concord Grape–Sage
CAIPIRINHA

This is a very seasonal drink because Concord grapes have such a short season. If you ever see them in the grocery store or farmer's market, grab them while they last!

5 **Concord grapes**, seeded

2 **sage leaves** or **thyme sprigs**, plus 1 for garnish

4 **lime wedges**

1 ounce **simple syrup** (see page 7)

2 ounces **cachaça**

In a rocks glass, muddle the grapes with 2 of the sage leaves, lime wedges, and simple syrup. Add the cachaça and fill with ice. Pour into a cocktail shaker and shake vigorously. Pour back into the rocks glass. Add additional ice, if needed. Garnish with the remaining sage leaf and serve.

Piña-Coconut CAIPIRINHA

Not as heavy as an authentic Piña Colada, but just as delicious and a little more tart.

¼ cup fresh **pineapple chunks**, plus wedge for garnish

4 **lime wedges**

1 ounce **coconut syrup**

2 ounces **cachaça**

Coconut chunks or **shredded coconut**, for garnish (optional)

In a rocks glass, muddle the pineapple with the lime wedges and coconut syrup. Add the cachaça and top with ice. Pour into a cocktail shaker and shake vigorously. Pour back into the rocks glass. Garnish with the pineapple wedge and coconut.

Guava Squeeze CAIPIRINHA

3 **lime wedges**

2 ruby **red grapefruit wedges**

1 ounce **simple syrup** (see page 7)

1 ounce Cruzan Guava **rum**

1 ounce **cachaça**

In a rocks glass, muddle the lime wedges with the grapefruit wedges and simple syrup. Add the rum and cachaça. Top with ice. Pour into a cocktail shaker. Shake vigorously. Pour back into the rocks glass.

30

Elderflower-Rosemary
CAIPIROSKA

4 **lemon wedges**, plus wheel for garnish

1 ounce **simple syrup** (see page 7)

1 sprig **rosemary**

1½ ounces **citrus vodka**

½ ounce St-Germain **elderflower liqueur**

In a cocktail shaker, muddle the lemon wedges with the simple syrup and rosemary. Add the vodka and elderflower liqueur. Top with ice and shake vigorously. Strain into a rocks glass filled with ice. Garnish with the lemon wheel. Scoop out the muddled rosemary sprig from the shaker and drop into the drink for additional garnish.

31

Kumquat CAIPIROSKA

Created by Master Mixologist (aka "Mister Mojito")
David Nepove.

5 or 6 ripe **kumquats**

2 teaspoons **sugar**

2 ounces SKYY Infusions **citrus vodka**

In a mixing glass, muddle the kumquats with the sugar. (Be sure to pulverize the kumquats.) Add the vodka and top with ice. Shake vigorously and pour into a rocks glass.

MUDDLED LIME, ORANGE, & LEMONADES

These are some simple recipes that use a combination of various muddled fruits and sweeteners along with lemonade. I use a lot of different herbs in these—but a little goes a long way and really adds a nice bouquet to the drink.

32

Strawberry-Basil
LEMONADE

3 ripe **strawberries**, hulled and sliced, plus 1 for garnish

2 **basil leaves**, plus 1 for garnish

1½ ounces fresh **lemon juice**

1½ ounces **simple syrup** (see page 7)

1½ ounces **water**

1½ ounces **citrus vodka**

In a mixing glass, muddle 3 of the strawberries with 2 of the basil leaves, the lemon juice, simple syrup, and water. Add the vodka and top with ice. Shake vigorously and pour into a tall glass. Garnish with the remaining strawberry and basil leaf.

33/34

Pineapple-Sage LIMEADE

¼ cup fresh **pineapple chunks**, plus wedge for garnish

1 **sage leaf**, plus 1 for garnish

1½ ounces fresh **lime juice**

1½ ounces **simple syrup** (see page 7)

1½ ounces **water**

¾ ounce SKYY Infusions **pineapple vodka**

¾ ounce **Midori**

In a mixing glass, muddle the pineapple chunks with 1 sage leaf, lime juice, simple syrup, and water. Add the vodka and Midori. Top with ice and shake vigorously. Pour into a cocktail glass. Garnish with the pineapple wedge and remaining sage leaf.

Muddled Grape LIMEADE

5 **red seedless grapes**, plus extra for garnish

5 **green seedless grapes**, plus extra for garnish

1 ounce fresh **lime juice**

1 ounce **simple syrup** (see page 7)

1 ounce **water**

1½ ounces **grape flavored vodka** (i.e. SKYY Infusions Grape or Three Olives Grape)

In a mixing glass, muddle the 5 red and 5 green grapes with the lime juice, simple syrup, and water. Add the vodka and top with ice. Shake vigorously and pour into a tall glass. Garnish with the remaining grapes.

35/36

Jalapeño ORANGEADE

4 **orange wedges**, plus wheel for garnish

1 teaspoon chopped **jalapeño**, plus slice for garnish

1 ounce fresh **lemon juice**

1 ounce **simple syrup** (see page 7)

1 ounce **water**

1½ ounces **citrus vodka**

In a cocktail shaker, muddle the orange wedges with the chopped jalapeño, lemon juice, simple syrup, and water. Add the vodka and top with ice. Shake vigorously and pour into a tall glass. Garnish with the orange wheel and jalapeño slice.

Watermelon-Basil LEMONADE

⅓ cup fresh **watermelon chunks**, plus wedge for garnish

2 **basil leaves**, plus 1 for garnish

1 ounce fresh **lemon juice**

1 ounce **simple syrup** (see page 7)

1 ounce **water**

¾ ounce **watermelon liqueur** (such as Pucker)

¾ ounce premium **vodka**

In a mixing glass, muddle the watermelon chunks with 2 of the basil leaves, the lemon juice, simple syrup, and water. Add the watermelon liqueur and vodka. Top with ice and shake vigorously. Pour into a tall glass and garnish with the watermelon wedge and remaining basil leaf.

Honeydew LEMONADE

¼ cup fresh **honeydew melon** or **cantaloupe chunks**

1 ounce fresh **lemon juice**

1 ounce **honey water** (see page 8)

1 ounce **water**

¾ ounce **Midori**

¾ ounce premium **vodka**

In a mixing glass, muddle the honeydew chunks with the lemon juice, honey water, and water. Add the Midori and vodka. Top with ice and shake vigorously. Pour into a tall glass.

Grapefruit-Honey
LEMONADE

4 ruby **red grapefruit wedges**, plus wheel for garnish

1 ounce fresh **lemon juice**

1 ounce **honey water** (see page 8)

1 ounce **water**

1½ ounces Belvedere **Pink Grapefruit vodka**

In a cocktail shaker, muddle the grapefruit wedges with the lemon juice, honey water, and water. Add the vodka. Top with ice and shake vigorously. Strain into a tall glass filled with fresh ice. Garnish with the grapefruit wheel.

39

Ginger Star

1 **star fruit slice**, plus 1 for garnish

¼ cup chopped fresh **green apple**

4 slices peeled fresh **ginger**

1 ounce fresh **lime juice**

1 ounce **simple syrup** (see page 7)

1½ ounces **citrus vodka**

Splash of **7-Up**

In a cocktail shaker, muddle 1 slice of the star fruit with the apple, ginger, lime juice, and simple syrup. Add the vodka. Top with ice and shake vigorously. Pour into a tall glass. Top with the 7-Up. Garnish with the remaining star fruit slice.

40/41

Classic Bourbon SMASH

4 **lemon wedges**

1 ounce **simple syrup** (see page 7)

4 or 5 **mint leaves**, plus sprig for garnish

2 ounces **whiskey** or **bourbon**

In a rocks glass, muddle the lemon wedges with the simple syrup and mint leaves. Add the whiskey and top with ice. Pour into a cocktail shaker and shake vigorously. Strain into the rocks glass and top with ice. Garnish with the mint sprig.

Grand SMASH

Because Grand Marnier is really a cognac infused with orange peels and other spices, it works beautifully in a classic Smash recipe. For those of you that are big "Grandma" (a nickname for Grand Marnier) fans, this is your drink. It tastes like an adult lemonade and is not too sweet.

5 **lemon wedges**

4 or 5 **mint leaves**, plus sprig for garnish

1¾ ounces **Grand Marnier** (for a luxurious version, use the Grand Marnier 100th or 150th anniversary editions)

In a rocks glass, muddle the lemon wedges with the mint leaves. Add the Grand Marnier and top with ice. Pour into a cocktail shaker and shake vigorously. Strain over fresh ice into the rocks glass. Garnish with the mint sprig.

42

Raspberry Smash

4 ripe **raspberries**, plus 1 for garnish

4 **lemon wedges**

1 ounce **raspberry syrup** (such as Monin) or **simple syrup** (see page 7)

4 or 5 **mint leaves**, plus sprig for garnish

2 ounces **cognac**

In a rocks glass, muddle 4 of the raspberries with the lemon wedges, raspberry syrup, and mint leaves. Add the cognac and top with ice. Pour into a cocktail shaker and shake vigorously. Strain over fresh ice in the rocks glass. Garnish with the mint sprig and remaining raspberry.

43

Strawberry-Basil SMASH

2 ripe **strawberries**, hulled, plus 1 for garnish

4 **lemon wedges**

2 **basil leaves**, plus 1 for garnish

1 ounce **simple syrup** (see page 7)

1½ ounces **gin** (Plymouth is a good choice)

In a cocktail shaker, muddle 2 of the strawberries with the lemon wedges, 2 of the basil leaves, and the simple syrup. Add the gin. Top with ice and shake vigorously. Strain into a rocks glass filled with fresh ice. Garnish with the remaining strawberry and basil leaf.

44/45

Conquistador SMASH

Made with a dry sherry and fresh, ripe cherries.

4 ripe Bing **cherries**, pitted, plus 1 for garnish

4 **lemon wedges**

1 ounce **simple syrup** (see page 7)

4 **mint leaves**, plus sprig for garnish

1½ ounces **dry sherry**

In a mixing glass, muddle the cherries with the lemon wedges, simple syrup, and mint leaves. Add the sherry and top with ice. Shake vigorously. Strain into a tall glass filled with fresh ice. Garnish with the remaining cherry and mint sprig.

Blackberry-Grappa SMASH

Made with grappa and fresh blackberries. (You can also just make a simple grappa Smash without the blackberries.)

4 ripe **blackberries**, plus 1 for garnish

4 **lemon wedges**

1 ounce **simple syrup** (see page 7)

4 **mint leaves**, plus sprig for garnish

1½ ounces **grappa**

In a cocktail shaker, muddle the blackberries with the lemon wedges, simple syrup, and mint leaves. Add the grappa and top with ice. Shake vigorously. Strain into a rocks glass filled with fresh ice. Garnish with the remaining blackberry and mint sprig.

Old Fashioned

Purportedly invented in the mid 1880s in Kentucky, there is some debate on whether the classic recipe actually muddles fruit or just uses a large piece of orange peel for the garnish. Personally, I like the muddled-fruit version, for I think it adds more flavor.

1 **sugar cube**

2 dashes of **bitters**

1 **orange wheel**, cut into quarters

1 **cherry**, pitted

2 ounces **bourbon** or **rye whiskey**

1 large piece of **orange peel**, for garnish

In a rocks glass, muddle the sugar cube with the bitters, orange, and cherry, adding a few drops of water to help dissolve the sugar, if needed. Add the bourbon and stir well. With a spoon, scoop out the muddled fruit and discard. Add 1 large ice cube. Garnish with the orange peel.

Añejo Old Fashioned

Same recipe as above, but use a good añejo tequila (like Gran Centenario or Don Julio) instead of the whiskey.

48

French Maid

From Jim Meehan of PDT in New York City.

3 **cucumber slices**, plus 1 for garnish

6 to 8 **mint leaves**, plus sprig for garnish

¾ ounce **simple syrup** (see page 7)

¾ ounce fresh **lime juice**

1½ ounces Hine V.S.O.P. **cognac**

¼ ounce John D. Taylor's **Velvet Falernum**

1 ounce **ginger beer**

Add 3 of the cucumber slices, the mint leaves, and simple syrup to a mixing glass and muddle. Add everything else, shake with ice, and strain into a Collins glass filled with ice. Garnish with the mint sprig poking through the remaining cucumber slice.

49

Super-Sonic Mango-Peach MASH-UP

A friend of mine, Bret Miller from Sherman, Texas, created this little mash-up that has long since become a tradition for his New Year's Eve parties. He, along with many others, knows the importance of ice. Wanting a specific type of ice for this drink, he bribes the counter guys at Sonic into giving him a few bags of their crushed ice. Nice.

1 ounce **mango puree** (or 2–3 slices fresh mango)

¼ cup peeled fresh **peach chunks**

1 ounce fresh **lime juice**

1 ounce **simple syrup** (see page 7)

1¼ ounces **light rum** or Cruzan Mango **rum**

Homemade **whipped cream**, for garnish (optional)

In a highball glass, muddle the mango with the peach chunks, lime juice, and simple syrup. Add the rum. Top with crushed ice. Stir well from the bottom up. Garnish with the whipped cream, if desired.

50/51

Lychee CRUSH

3 **lychee nuts** (fresh is best, but canned lychees will also work)

1 ounce fresh **lemon juice**

1 ounce **lemongrass syrup** (such as Monin) or simple syrup (see page 7; if using canned lychees, you can use the syrup from the can)

1½ ounces Grey Goose La Poire **vodka**

Splash of **soda water**

Thin strand of **lemongrass** or **lemon wheel**, for garnish

In a cocktail shaker, muddle the lychee nuts with the lemon juice and lemongrass syrup. (The lychee nuts should be muddled to a pulp.) Add the vodka. Top with ice and shake vigorously. Strain into a tall glass filled with fresh ice. Top with the soda water and stir well. Garnish with the strand of lemongrass.

Granny Smith

Created by Master Mixologist (aka "Mister Mojito") David Nepove.

¼ cup peeled fresh **green apple chunks**, plus slice for garnish

½ ounce fresh **lemon juice**

½ ounce **simple syrup** (see page 7)

1½ ounces **vodka**

1 ounce **apple schnapps** or **dessert wine**

¼ ounce **apple brandy** or **eau de vie**

In a mixing glass, muddle the apple chunks with the lemon juice and simple syrup. Add the vodka, schnapps, and brandy. Fill with ice, shake vigorously, and strain into a chilled martini glass. Garnish with the apple slice.

COBBLER

A cobbler is simply muddled fruit with sugar and a spirit base—a pretty broad definition that encompasses just about anything you can muddle.

52

Blackberry COBBLER

5 ripe **blackberries**, plus extra for garnish

10 ripe **blueberries**

1 ounce fresh **lemon juice**

1 ounce **simple syrup** (see page 7)

1½ ounces **gin** (such as Hendrick's or Tanqueray No. Ten)

½ ounce **crème de cassis**

Splash of **champagne** (best with demi-sec or semi-sweet sparkling wine)

In a mixing glass, muddle 5 of the blackberries with the blueberries, lemon juice, and simple syrup. Add the gin and crème de cassis. Top with ice and shake vigorously. Pour into a tall glass and top with the champagne. Stir from the bottom up. Garnish with the remaining blackberries.

53

Wild Raspberry COBBLER

6 ripe **raspberries**, plus 1 for garnish

4 **mint leaves**, plus sprig for garnish

1 ounce fresh **lemon juice**

1 ounce **simple syrup** (see page 7)

1 ounce **gin** (such as Hendrick's)

½ ounce **raspberry liqueur** (such as Mathilde)

Splash of **rosé champagne** (optional)

In a cocktail shaker, muddle 6 of the raspberries with the mint leaves, lemon juice, and simple syrup. Add the gin and raspberry liqueur. Top with ice and shake vigorously. Pour into a tall glass. Add additional ice, if needed, and top with the champagne, if desired. Stir well. Garnish with the remaining raspberry and mint sprig.

54

Grand Marnier & BERRIES

A classic dessert made into a cocktail.

½ cup ripe seasonal **berries** (such as hulled strawberries, blueberries, raspberries, etc.), plus extra for garnish

1 ounce fresh **lemon juice**

1 ounce **simple syrup** (see page 7; if using berries that are not that sweet, add more simple syrup to taste)

1¼ ounces **Grand Marnier**

Splash of **champagne**

In a mixing glass, muddle the berries with the lemon juice and simple syrup, adding additional syrup, if needed. Add the Grand Marnier. Top with ice and shake vigorously. Pour into a tall glass. Top with the champagne and stir. Garnish with the remaining berries.

55

Strawberry COBBLER

3 ripe **strawberries**, hulled, plus 1 for garnish

1 ounce fresh **lemon juice**

1 ounce **simple syrup** (see page 7)

½ ounce Navan **vanilla liqueur**

1½ ounces premium **vodka** or gin (if preferred)

Splash of **soda water** or **champagne** (for a luxurious version)

In a mixing glass, muddle 3 of the strawberries with the lemon juice and simple syrup. Add the vanilla liqueur and vodka. Top with ice and shake vigorously. Pour into a tall glass. Top with the soda water. Stir and garnish with the remaining strawberry.

56

Cucumber GIMLET

This is one of my all-time favorite cocktails, a fresh gimlet versus the "classic" gimlet, which is made from preserved lime juice. (Why preserved lime juice you ask? Long story about sailors and scurvy. . .) I always use Hendrick's gin in this cocktail because of its light and fresh floral notes, which play so well with cucumber.

7 to 10 hothouse **cucumber slices**, plus extra for garnish

1 ounce fresh **lime juice**

1 ounce **simple syrup** (see page 7)

2 ounces **gin** (such as Hendrick's)

In a mixing glass, muddle 7 to 10 of the cucumber slices with the lime juice and simple syrup. Add the gin. Top with ice and shake vigorously. Strain into a chilled martini glass or over fresh ice in a rocks glass. Garnish with the remaining cucumber slices.

57

Seasonal Cucumber GIMLET

I also call this one a "Meglet," named after my good friend Meg, who is fond of gin and cucumber. This is a classic fresh gimlet—lime juice and gin—but muddled with cucumber and *one* other seasonal ingredient (see suggestions below). It's good anytime of year. I recommend using a lighter, more feminine gin like Hendrick's.

7 to 10 hothouse **cucumber slices**, plus extra for garnish

Add any *one* of the following seasonal ingredients—all go well with cucumber:

SPRING: organic rose petals; fresh herbs (such as basil, cilantro, sage, mint, thyme, etc.)

SUMMER: 1 strawberry; 3 raspberries; ¼ cup fresh cantaloupe chunks ; ¼ cup fresh watermelon chunks; 1 kiwi, peeled and cut into chunks

FALL: 2 kumquats; ¼ cup fresh peach chunks; ¼ cup fresh plum chunks

WINTER: 3 tablespoons pomegranate seeds; 6 to 7 tangerine wedges; ¼ cup fresh pear and apple chunks

1 ounce fresh **lime juice**

1 ounce **simple syrup** (see page 7)

2 ounces **gin** (such as Hendrick's)

In a mixing glass, muddle 7 to 10 of the cucumber slices with the seasonal ingredient of your choice, the lime juice, and simple syrup. Add the gin and top with ice. Shake vigorously. You can either strain into a chilled martini glass or strain into a rocks glass over fresh ice. Garnish with the remaining cucumber slices and a piece of seasonal fruit and serve.

58

Spiced Basil MIMOSA

Created by Angie Jackson, a mixologist based in Chicago, Illinois.

2 **orange wedges**

3 **basil leaves**, plus 1 for garnish

¾ ounce **ginger honey syrup** (recipe below)

1 ounce **citrus vodka**

½ ounce **orange curaçao** or **triple sec**

Splash of **sparkling white wine**

In a mixing glass, muddle the orange wedges with 3 of the basil leaves and the ginger honey syrup. Add the vodka and orange curaçao. Top with ice and shake vigorously. Either strain into a champagne flute or strain into a highball glass filled with fresh ice. Top with the sparkling wine. Garnish with the remaining basil leaf.

Ginger Honey Syrup

1 cup **water**

1 cup **sugar**

1 tablespoon **honey**

¼ cup cubed peeled fresh **ginger**

In a medium saucepan, heat the water over medium heat and stir in the sugar. Cook, stirring, until the sugar is dissolved. Add the honey and stir well. Add the ginger and remove from heat. Steep for 45 minutes. Remove and discard ginger and strain syrup into a bottle. Keep refrigerated until ready to use.

59

Burning Passion
MARGARITA

A very flavor-forward Margarita made with a passion fruit puree and hint of heat from the jalapeño. Sooooo good.

½ ripe **passion fruit** or 1 ounce passion fruit puree

½ teaspoon of chopped seeded **jalapeño** (or more to taste), plus 1 slice for garnish

1 ounce fresh **lime juice**

½ ounce fresh **lemon juice**

1 ounce **agave nectar** or 1½ ounces **simple syrup** (see page 7)

1½ ounces **silver tequila**

¾ ounce **triple sec**

Lime wheel, for garnish

In a mixing glass, muddle the passion fruit with the chopped jalapeño, lime juice, lemon juice, and agave nectar. Add the tequila and triple sec. Top with ice and shake vigorously. Strain into a rocks glass over fresh ice. Garnish with the jalapeño slice and lime wheel.

60
Kiwi-Coconut CRUSH

1 **kiwi**, peeled and cut into chunks

½ ounce fresh **lime juice**

½ ounce **coconut syrup**

½ ounce **Midori**

½ ounce **vodka**

½ ounce **coconut rum**

½ ounce **coconut milk**

In a mixing glass, muddle the kiwi with the lime juice and coconut syrup. Add the Midori, vodka, coconut rum, and coconut milk. Top with ice and shake vigorously. Pour into a rocks glass.

61

Pink Peppermelon
MARGARITA

I created this one at Aspen Food & Wine one year.
It was paired with a watermelon and crab gazpacho
and was a big hit. X-Rated is a mango, passion fruit,
blood orange liqueur.

2 tablespoons **pink peppercorns**, for garnishing rim

4 tablespoons **kosher salt**, for garnishing rim

Lime wedge

½ cup fresh **watermelon chunks**

1 teaspoon chopped seeded **jalapeño** (or more to taste)

1 ounce fresh **lime juice**

1 ounce **simple syrup** (see page 7)

2 ounces reposado **tequila** (such as Cabo Wabo Reposado)

½ ounce **Cointreau**

½ ounce **X-Rated liqueur**

Crush the peppercorns in a mortar and pestle. Place in a bowl
and mix with the salt. When ready to rim the glasses, wet the
outside rim of each glass with the lime wedge and dip into the
salt and peppercorn mixture. Set the rimmed glasses aside.

In a mixing glass, muddle the watermelon with the jalapeño,
lime juice, and simple syrup. Add the tequila, Cointreau, and X-
Rated liqueur. Top with ice and shake vigorously. Fill the rimmed
glass with ice and strain into the glass.

62

Muddled Avocado
MARGARITA

Most people think, "Avocado? In a drink?" Avocado is a great textural element in a drink; it adds a nice creaminess, but without the cream. It's especially good in a Margarita and goes REALLY well with chips and salsa. The avocado flavor is not overpowering. It's more like a great Margarita with a creamy element to it. The key to this drink is the salt. I'm not a huge fan of salt with my Margaritas, but this drink needs it. And if you want to get a little crazy, add some celery salt and crushed green peppercorns to the salt garnish.

Lime wedge

Kosher salt, for garnishing rim

¼ cup fresh **avocado chunks**

1 tablespoon chopped **cilantro** (optional)

1 ounce fresh **lime juice**

1 ounce **simple syrup** (see page 7)

1½ ounces reposado **tequila**

¾ ounce **triple sec**

Lime wedge, for garnish

Wet the outside rim of a rocks glass with the lime wedge. Dip rim into the salt and set aside.

In a mixing glass, muddle the avocado with the cilantro, lime juice, and simple syrup. Add the tequila and triple sec. Top with ice and shake vigorously. Strain over fresh ice in the rimmed rocks glass. Garnish with the lime wedge.

Big Plum

1 ripe **plum**, pitted and cut into chunks, plus wedge for garnish

1 ounce fresh **lime juice**

1 ounce **simple syrup** (see page 7)

1 ounce Hendrick's **gin** or **vodka** (if preferred)

½ ounce **crème de cassis**

Splash of **soda water**

In a tall glass, muddle the plum with the lime juice and simple syrup. Add the gin and crème de cassis. Top with ice. Pour into a cocktail shaker and shake vigorously. Pour back into the tall glass. Add additional ice, if needed. Top with the soda water and stir. Garnish with the plum wedge.

Kumquat Fresca
MARGARITA

4 or 5 hothouse **cucumber slices**

3 ripe **kumquats**, cut in half

4 **cilantro leaves** (optional)

1 ounce fresh **lime juice**

1 ounce **simple syrup** (see page 7)

1½ ounces silver **tequila**

¾ ounce **triple sec**

In a tall glass, muddle the cucumber slices with the kumquats, cilantro, if desired, lime juice, and simple syrup. Add the tequila and triple sec and top with ice. Shake vigorously. Serve immediately.

MUDDLED MARTINIS

These are some cocktails that require muddling, but are strained and served straight up. What a difference the fresh fruit makes, even in the simples of cocktails such as the Cosmopolitan.

65

Cosmo Fresh

A fresh, muddled variation on the classic Cosmopolitan.

4 **lime wedges**

½ ounce **simple syrup** (see page 7)

1 ounce **cranberry juice**

1½ ounces **citrus vodka** (best if using an infused or macerated vodka like SKYY Infusions or Belvedere Citrus)

¾ ounce **triple sec**

Lime twist, for garnish

In a mixing glass, muddle the lime wedges with the simple syrup and cranberry juice. Add the vodka and triple sec. Top with ice and shake vigorously. Strain into a chilled martini glass. Garnish with the lime twist and serve.

66/67

Passion Fruit LEMON DROP

The oils off the muddled lemon wedges make this martini explode with flavor.

4 **lemon wedges**

1 ounce **simple syrup** (see page 7)

2 ounces SKYY Infusions **passion fruit vodka**

Lemon peel, for garnish

In a mixing glass, muddle the lemon wedges with the simple syrup. Add the vodka and top with ice. Shake vigorously and strain into a chilled martini glass. Garnish with the lemon peel.

Black Raspberry MARTINI

4 **raspberries**, plus 1 for garnish

2 **blackberries**, plus 1 for garnish

1 ounce fresh **lime juice**

1 ounce **simple syrup** (see page 7)

2 ounces Belvedere **black raspberry vodka**

Splash of **rosé champagne** (optional)

In a mixing glass, muddle the 4 raspberries and 2 blackberries with the lime juice and simple syrup. Add the vodka and top with ice. Shake vigorously. Strain into a chilled martini glass. Top with the champagne, if desired. Garnish with the remaining raspberry and blackberry.

White Lotus

6 to 8 hothouse **cucumber slices**, plus 1 for garnish

1/2 ounce **simple syrup** (see page 7)

1/2 ounce fresh **lime juice**

3/4 ounce premium **vodka** (such as Chopin)

3/4 ounce Hendrick's **gin**

1/2 ounce St-Germain **elderflower liqueur** (if using simple syrup)

White orchid, for garnish

In a mixing glass, muddle the 6 to 8 cucumber slices with the elderflower syrup and lime juice. Add the vodka, gin, and elder-flower liqueur, if using. Top with ice and shake vigorously. Strain into a rocks glass filled with ice. Garnish with the white orchid and remaining cucumber slice.

Apple 'n' Sage MARTINI

Years ago, the apple martini was all the rage. This fresh version has more layers of flavor and is bursting with freshness.

1/4 cup chopped peeled fresh green **apple**

1 **sage leaf**, plus 1 for garnish

1/2 ounce fresh **lime juice**

1/2 ounce **simple syrup** (see page 7)

1 1/4 ounces premium **vodka** (SKYY Infusions ginger vodka is a good choice here. It gives the drink a subtle spiciness.)

3/4 ounce **apple liqueur** (such as Puckers or Marie Brizard Manzanita)

In a mixing glass, muddle the apple with 1 sage leaf, the lime juice, and simple syrup. Muddle until the apple is pulverized. Add the vodka and apple liqueur. Top with ice and shake vigorously. Strain into a chilled martini glass. Garnish with the remaining sage leaf.

70

Gingered Pear

Created by my friend, Debbi Peek, a mixologist from Chicago, Illinois.

Ground **ginger** and **sugar**, for garnishing rim (optional)

Lemon wedge

½ ripe **pear**, cored and chopped

1 ounce fresh **lemon juice**

½ ounce **maple syrup**

1½ ounces Grey Goose La Poire **vodka**

½ ounce Domaine de Canton **ginger liqueur**

If you'd like to garnish the rim, combine sugar and ginger on a small plate. Wet the rim of a martini glass with the lemon wedge and dip the rim in the sugar mixture to coat. Set aside. In a mixing glass, muddle the pear, lemon juice, and maple syrup. Add the vodka, ginger liqueur, and ice and shake. Strain into the rimmed martini glass.

71

Hana Meadow

A bartender at the Four Seasons Resort Maui created this one during one of my training visits. It's one of their most popular cocktails.

- 4 ruby red **grapefruit wedges**, plus wheel for garnish
- 2 **basil leaves**, plus 1 for garnish
- ½ ounce **simple syrup** (see page 7)
- ¾ ounce Absolut Ruby Red **vodka**
- ½ ounce **gin** (such as Tanqueray Rangpur)

In a mixing glass, muddle the grapefruit wedges with 2 of the basil leaves and the simple syrup. Add the vodka and gin. Top with ice and shake vigorously. Strain into a chilled martini glass or strain into a rocks glass with fresh ice. Garnish with the grapefruit wheel and remaining basil leaf.

72/73

White Grape MARTINI

10 white seedless **grapes**, plus extra for garnish

4 **lemon wedges**

1 ounce **simple syrup** (see page 7)

2 ounces **grape-flavored vodka** (i.e. SKYY Infusions Grape or Three Olives Grape)

In a mixing glass, muddle 10 of the grapes with the lemon wedges and simple syrup. Add the vodka. Top with ice and shake vigorously. Strain into a chilled martini glass. Garnish with speared white grapes.

Strawberry-Balsamic CRUSH

2 ripe **strawberries**, hulled, plus 1 for garnish

1 teaspoon aged **balsamic vinegar**

½ ounce fresh **lime juice**

1 ounce **simple syrup** (see page 7)

1½ ounces premium **vodka**

Freshly ground **black pepper** (optional)

In a mixing glass, muddle 2 of the strawberries with the vinegar, lime juice, and simple syrup. Add the vodka and top with ice. Shake vigorously. Either strain into a rocks glass over fresh ice or into a chilled martini glass. Top with a twist of fresh ground black pepper, if desired. Garnish with the remaining strawberry.

74

Mekong Pear

¼ cup peeled fresh Bartlett **pear chunks**, plus sliver for garnish

3 slices **cucumber**, plus 1 for garnish

1 ounce fresh **lime juice**

1 ounce **simple syrup** (see page 7)

1¼ ounces Belvedere **vodka**

¾ ounce dry **sake**

Splash of **gin**

In a mixing glass, muddle the pear chunks and 3 of the cucumber slices with the lime juice and simple syrup. Add the vodka, sake and gin. Top with ice and shake vigorously. Strain into a chilled martini glass. Garnish with the pear sliver and remaining cucumber slice.

75/76

Sangria SMASH

4 **orange wedges**, plus wheel for garnish

1 ripe **strawberry**, hulled and sliced, plus 1 for garnish

Dash of ground **cinnamon**

1 ounce **simple syrup** (see page 7)

½ ounce **Grand Marnier**

3 ounces hearty **red wine** (i.e. syrah, cabernet, rioja, etc.)

1 ounce **Sprite**

In a cocktail shaker, muddle the orange wedges with 1 strawberry, cinnamon, and simple syrup. Add the Grand Marnier and red wine. Top with ice and shake vigorously. Strain into a wineglass filled with fresh ice. Add the Sprite and garnish with the orange wheel and remaining strawberry.

Ruby Red Sangria SMASH

4 ruby red **grapefruit wedges**, plus quarter-wheel for garnish

2 **lemon wedges**

4 **mint leaves**, plus sprig for garnish

1½ ounces **simple syrup** (see page 7)

3 ounces **white wine** (such as sauvignon blanc)

Splash of **Sprite**

In a cocktail shaker, muddle the grapefruit wedges with the lemon wedges, mint leaves, and simple syrup. Add the wine and top with ice. Shake vigorously. Strain into a wineglass filled with fresh ice. Top with the Sprite. Garnish with the grapefruit quarter-wheel and mint sprig.

77

Embittered Italian

2 **blood orange wedges**, plus wheel for garnish

2 **lemon wedges**

1 ounce **simple syrup** (see page 7)

¼ ounce **Campari**

½ ounce **gin**

Splash of **Prosecco**

In a mixing glass, muddle the orange and lemon wedges with the simple syrup. Add the Campari and gin. Top with ice and shake vigorously. Strain into a tall glass over fresh ice. Top with the Prosecco and stir. Garnish with the blood orange wheel.

78

Southern Belle PICK

A Pick is a classic southern drink made of vodka and iced tea. This is a souped-up version with fresh peaches . . . mmmmm, peaches.

¼ cup peeled fresh **peach chunks**

1 ounce **simple syrup** (see page 7)

1 ounce fresh **lemon juice**

3 ounces brewed black **tea** (such as orange pekoe), chilled or at room temperature

1¼ ounces Absolut Apeach **vodka**

Mint sprig, for garnish

In a mixing glass, muddle the peach chunks with the simple syrup and lemon juice. Add the tea and vodka. Top with ice and shake vigorously. Strain into a tall glass filled with fresh ice. Garnish with the mint sprig and serve.

79

Muddled Mary

From my friend, Phil Adler, the head mixologist at the corporate office of The Cheesecake Factory. I was salivating when he sent this one to me!

Lime wedge

One 1-inch piece **red bell pepper**

1 thin slice **serrano chile**, seeded

⅛ teaspoon **tomato paste**

Five ¼-inch slices **celery**

Pinch of **paprika**

Pinch of **kosher salt**

Pinch of **celery salt**

⅛ teaspoon fresh cracked **black pepper** (extra for rim)

1½ ounces **vodka** or silver **tequila** (for a "Muddled Maria")

1½ ounces **tomato juice**

Prep: To rim an 8-ounce martini glass or flared champagne flute, wet the outside rim with a lime wedge. Dip the rim into the salt and pepper mixture to coat and set aside.

In a mixing glass, combine the bell pepper, serrano chile, tomato paste, celery, paprika, pinch of kosher salt, celery salt, and the ⅛ teaspoon black pepper. Muddle well. Add the vodka, tomato juice, and about ½ cup ice. Shake for a good 20 to 30 seconds. Strain into the rimmed glass.

VARIATIONS: There are several herbs and spices that work really well with this fresh Bloody Mary. Add one or more of the ingredients below to the muddled mixture to "spice up" the recipe a bit.
Asian: Two quarter-size slices of peeled fresh ginger or ¼ teaspoon wasabi paste
Spiced: ⅛ teaspoon ground cumin
Italian or Herb: 2 large basil leaves

Clockwork Orange

4 **orange wedges** (such as navel, tangerine, or a combination of different oranges, if desired), plus wheel for garnish

1 teaspoon **dark brown sugar**

½ ounce fresh **lemon juice**

1 ounce orange **vodka**

½ ounce Cruzan Guava **rum**

Splash of **soda water**

In a mixing glass, muddle the orange wedges with the sugar and lemon juice. Add the vodka and rum. Top with ice and shake vigorously. Pour into a rocks glass. Top with the soda water and stir. Garnish with the orange wheel.

Kumquat-Ginger COOLER

3 ripe **kumquats**

1 ounce fresh **lemon juice**

1 ounce **simple syrup** (see page 7)

1 ounce **citrus vodka**

1 ounce Domaine de Canton **ginger liqueur**

Splash of **soda water**

In a mixing glass, muddle the kumquats with the lemon juice and simple syrup. Add the vodka and ginger liqueur. Top with ice and shake vigorously. Pour into a tall glass and add additional ice, if needed. Top with the soda water and stir.

82

Scandinavian Sweet
SWIZZLE

My in-laws make this traditional Scandinavian dish over the holidays called "Sweet Soup" (aka "Dried Fruit Soup")—it's a cold soup made with dried fruits such as apricots, raisins, and cherries cooked with water and fruit juice, then cooled. This is my souped-up cocktail version. I'd recommend serving these in nice tall shot glasses or even port glasses.

½ cup **Sweet Soup** (recipe below), including the fruit

1 ounce **port**

½ ounce **aquavit**

In a mixing glass, muddle the Sweet Soup and fruit pieces. Add the port and aquavit. Top with ice and shake vigorously. Strain into a port glass.

Sweet Soup
Makes 6 cups or enough for 18 cocktails

5 cups of **water**

½ cup chopped **dried apples**

½ cup **dark raisins**

½ cup **golden raisins**

½ cup **dried apricots**

½ cup **prunes**, pitted

2 dashes ground **cinnamon**

1 cup **apple** or **cranberry juice**

In a large saucepan, bring the water to a boil, then add the dried fruit and cinnamon. Simmer until the apricots and raisins really soften, about 15 minutes. Stir in the apple juice. Remove from the heat and let cool. Refrigerate until ready to use. This should keep for several days.

83

Poached Pear MARTINI

This is a perfect example of how you can literally muddle anything in a drink. Several years ago I was working with a restaurant group in Ohio and the chef had made these wonderful poached pears. They were racking their brains trying to figure out how to use a poached pear as a garnish in a cocktail for the holidays—everything from trying to balance it on the edge of the glass to having a chunk of it at the bottom of a martini glass to floating it. I told them to throw it in and muddle it in the cocktail! We made these gorgeous spiced pear martinis that were very popular for them. (But on the downside, I think the chef got upset because he ended up having to make about a hundred of these poached pears over the holidays.)

¼ poached **pear** (recipe on page 109 or you can use your own)

1 ounce **pear nectar**

1 ounce **cranberry juice**

½ ounce fresh **lemon juice**

½ ounce **simple syrup** (see page 7)

Pinch of **ground cinnamon**

¼ ounce **Grand Marnier**

1 ounce Belvedere **orange vodka**

In a mixing glass, muddle the poached pear with the pear nectar, cranberry juice, lemon juice, simple syrup, and ground cinnamon. Add the Grand Marnier and vodka. Top with ice and shake moderately. Strain into a chilled martini glass.

Poached Pears

Makes 6 cups or enough for 18 martinis

2 ripe **pears** (such as Bosc, Anjou, or Bartlett), peeled, cored, and cut into quarters

1 cup **red wine**

¼ cup **sugar**

1 tablespoon fresh **lemon juice**

In a saucepan, combine all the ingredients over medium heat until the mixture starts to simmer. Let poach until the pears become soft (a knife can be easily poked all the way through them), 3 to 4 minutes, then turn pears over to poach the other side. When fully cooked, take off the heat and let cool.

84/85

Banana EGG CREAM

½ ripe **banana**, peeled

6 **Nilla wafers**, plus extra for garnish (optional)

2 teaspoons **dark brown sugar**

1½ ounces **half-and-half**

¾ ounce Cruzan Banana **rum**

¾ ounce **dark rum**

Splash of **soda water**

In a mixing glass, muddle the banana and 6 Nilla wafers with the sugar and half-and-half. Add both rums. Top with ice and shake vigorously. Strain into a tall glass filled with ice. Top with the soda water and stir. Garnish with additional Nilla wafers, if desired.

Raspberry–Irish Cream CRUSH

7 ripe **raspberries**, plus 3 for garnish

3 ounces **Baileys Irish Cream**

Muddle 7 of the raspberries in the bottom of a rocks glass. Top with crushed ice. Fill with Baileys. (It will layer on top of the raspberries.) Garnish with the remaining 3 raspberries. Serve with a small spoon.

Muddled Russian

2 Oreo **cookies**

¾ ounce **Kahlúa**

¾ ounce **vodka**

1½ ounces **half-and-half**

In a rocks glass, muddle the cookies with the Kahlúa and vodka. Top with crushed ice. Top with half-and-half and stir slowly.

Bourbon-Peach JULEP

4 or 5 **mint leaves**, plus sprig for garnish

¼ cup fresh **peach chunks**, plus slice for garnish

1 ounce **simple syrup** (see page 7)

1½ ounces **bourbon**

½ ounce **peach liqueur**

In a tall glass, muddle the mint leaves with the peach chunks and simple syrup. Add the bourbon and peach liqueur. Top with crushed ice and stir for a good minute. (Keep adding crushed ice, as needed.) Garnish with the mint sprig and peach slice.

88

Classic Mint JULEP

A classic Mint Julep is a very simple recipe and goes down easily, yet one rarely gets a good one; it's usually too strong or too sweet. When I was first bartending, I kept trying to make this cocktail and would follow the recipe to the tee, but I always thought it was way too strong. It wasn't until years later when I was working at country club during the Kentucky Derby that I finally got it right. One of the patrons—who was from Kentucky—told me, "Miss! Slow down! This is a southern drink. We like it slow and easy, lots of ice." That was the trick! I think of this drink like how most southerners like their iced tea—a little on the sweet side, packed with lots and lots of ice, watered down but with a lot of flavor, and very cold. It's the same with a Mint Julep—it should be pretty watered down and very cold. It will take you a good 1 to 2 minutes to make a good one. Ideally, you should try and make it in either a glass or metal cup to keep it cool.

4 or 5 **mint leaves**, plus 1 sprig for garnish

1 ounce **simple syrup** (see page 7)

2 ounces premium **bourbon** (such as Woodford Reserve or Maker's Mark)

In a tall glass, lightly muddle the mint leaves with the simple syrup. Add the bourbon and pack with crushed ice. Stir the drink with a bar spoon—stir, stir, stir! Add more ice and keep stirring. Keep adding ice and stirring for a good minute. You know it's ready when frost starts to form on the outside of the glass. Garnish with the mint sprig and serve.

89/90

Lemon-Basil JULEP

From one of my good friends—Philip Raimondo, Master Mixologist, Beam Global Spirits & Wine.

2 **basil leaves**, plus 1 for garnish

1 ounce **simple syrup** (see page 7)

1 ounce fresh **lemon juice**

1 dash Fee Brothers **lemon bitters** (traditional bitters will also work)

2 ounces **bourbon** (such as Basil Hayden's or Maker's Mark) Lemon zest, for garnish

In a mixing glass, add 2 of the basil leaves and the simple syrup. Lightly muddle the basil leaves, but don't go crazy. Add the lemon juice, bitters, and bourbon and shake well with ice. Strain into a chilled martini glass or pour over fresh crushed ice in a highball glass. Garnish with the remaining basil leaf and lemon zest.

Bourbon-Cherry JULEP

I use a combination of a bourbon and a cherry vodka for a bigger burst of cherry flavor.

4 or 5 **mint leaves**, plus sprig for garnish

3 ripe Bing **cherries**, pitted, plus 1 for garnish

1 ounce **simple syrup** (see page 7)

¾ ounce **bourbon**

¾ ounce **cherry vodka** (i.e. SKYY Infusions or Three Olives)

In a cocktail glass, muddle the mint leaves with 3 of the cherries and the simple syrup. Add the bourbon and cherry vodka. Top with crushed ice and stir for a good minute. (Keep adding crushed ice, as needed.) Garnish with the mint sprig and remaining cherry.

Cranberry LEDERHOSEN

This drink uses a beer, specifically a Belgian lambic—full-bodied, a little sweet, and lots of fruit flavor. Tastes like a great holiday punch.

4 **mint leaves**, plus sprig for garnish

6 **cranberries**, plus 1 for garnish

1 ounce **simple syrup** (see page 7)

1 ounce **cognac**

2 ounces Belgian **lambic beer** (peach, passion fruit, or raspberry)

In a cocktail shaker, muddle the mint leaves with 6 of the cranberries and the simple syrup. Add the cognac. Top with ice and shake vigorously. Pour into a tall glass. Top off with the lambic and stir well. Garnish with the mint sprig and remaining cranberry.

Wild Berry JULEP

4 or 5 **mint leaves**, plus sprig for garnish

¼ cup seasonal **berries**, plus extra for garnish

1 ounce **simple syrup** (see page 7)

¾ ounce **bourbon**

¾ ounce SKYY Infusions **raspberry vodka**

In a cocktail glass, muddle the mint leaves with the ¼ cup seasonal berries and simple syrup. Top with crushed ice and stir for a good minute. (Keep adding crushed ice, as needed.) Garnish with the mint sprig and remaining berries.

93

Holiday Mint JULEP

Created by Matt Wallace, lead bartender at Seven Grand in Los Angeles.

- 6 to 10 **cranberries**, plus 1 for garnish
- 2 sprigs of **mint**, plus 1 for garnish
- ¾ ounce **spiced simple syrup** (recipe below)
- 2 ounces Woodford Reserve **bourbon**

In a cocktail glass or metal cup, muddle 6 to 10 of the cranberries with the 2 sprigs of mint and spiced simple syrup. Add the bourbon, top with crushed ice, and stir well. Add more crushed ice, if needed. Garnish with the remaining cranberry and mint sprig.

Spiced Simple Syrup

- 2 cups **water**
- 2 cups **sugar**
- 3 to 4 **cinnamon sticks**
- 2 **whole nutmegs** or 4 to 5 dashes **ground nutmeg**
- 4 to 5 whole **cloves**
- 1 **star anise**
- **Black peppercorns**, if desired

In a saucepan, combine all the ingredients and bring to a boil. Take off heat and let steep for at least a couple of hours or all day if you want it more potent. Keep covered and refrigerated until ready to use. This should keep for a week or so.

94/95

Spiced Cherry ZINGER

5 ripe Bing **cherries**, pitted, plus 1 for garnish

4 **mint leaves**

¾ ounce **spiced simple syrup** (see page 118)

1½ ounces **bourbon** (such as Jim Beam Black)

Splash of **Tuaca**

In a cocktail glass, muddle the cherries with the mint leaves and spiced simple syrup. Add the bourbon and Tuaca. Top with crushed ice and stir for a good 30 seconds. Garnish with the remaining cherry.

Vanilla Bean Bourbon PRESS

¼ **vanilla bean**, split in half

1 ounce **simple syrup** (see page 7)

Dash of **Angostura bitters**

1½ ounces **bourbon** (such as Maker's Mark)

In a mixing glass, muddle the vanilla bean with the simple syrup and bitters. Add the bourbon and top with crushed ice. Stir, stir, and stir for a good minute. Add more crushed ice if needed and keep stirring. Serve.

96

Inverno

The name of this drink means "winter" in both Italian and Portuguese. It is made with Cynar, an Italian apéritif made from artichokes. It sounds strange, but it's quite delicious.

Created by Tad Carducci of The Tippling Bros. for APO Bar + Lounge in Philadelphia.

2 **lime wedges**

2 **kumquats** or ½ tangerine

Heaping teaspoon of **dark brown sugar**

Pinch of **ground cinnamon**

1½ ounces Leblon **cachaça**

½ ounce **amaretto** (such as Luxardo)

¼ ounce **Cynar liqueur**

Cinnamon stick, for garnish

Bitters, for garnish (optional)

In a cocktail shaker, muddle the lime wedges with the kumquats, sugar, and ground cinnamon. Add the cachaça, amaretto, and Cynar and shake with ice. Pour into a double old-fashioned glass. Garnish with the cinnamon stick. For a cool effect, splash some bitters on one end of the cinnamon stick and hit it with a lighter for a few seconds. Drop the unlit end into the drink. It will burn for a few seconds and give off an amazing aroma.

97

Spiced Mango MOJITO

This is a great one for the fall months and the holiday season.

10 **mint leaves**, plus sprig for garnish

1 ounce **mango puree**

3 dashes of **ground cinnamon**

1 ounce fresh **lime juice**

1 ounce **simple syrup** (see page 7)

2 ounces premium **rum** (such as 10 Cane)

Splash of **soda water**

Cinnamon stick, for garnish

In a rocks or highball glass, muddle the mint leaves with the mango puree, ground cinnamon, lime juice, and simple syrup. Add the rum. Top with crushed ice and the soda water. Stir well and garnish with the mint sprig and cinnamon stick.

MUDDLED MOCKTAILS (NONALCOHOLIC)

I have two kids and my little boy, Holden, is always seeing me in the kitchen mixing away, often using my muddler. He says "Mommy, hit de fruit!" (We're teaching him not to hit his sister, but hitting fruit in a cup is okay.) So, while I'm creating concoctions for various clients, I usually end up making him a nonalcoholic version of whatever I'm doing. But, in the process, I've created quite a few great nonalcoholic "muddlers," as I call them. And, you can always add alcohol to them if you want because they are great bases with which to start.

98

Pineapple Pogo

¼ cup fresh **pineapple chunks**

¼ cup fresh **mango chunks**

1 ounce fresh **lime juice**

1 ounce **simple syrup** (see page 7)

Splash of **soda water**

In a cocktail shaker, muddle the pineapple and mango with the lime juice and simple syrup. Top with ice and shake. Pour into a tall glass, add the soda water, and stir well.

99/100

Lemon-Ginger FIZZY

4 **lemon wedges**

4 **mint leaves**, plus sprig for garnish

¾ ounce **agave nectar**

Splash of **ginger beer** or **ginger ale**

In a cocktail shaker, muddle the lemon wedges with the mint leaves and agave nectar. Top with ice and shake vigorously. Pour into a tall glass. Top with the ginger beer and stir. Garnish with the mint sprig.

5-Citrus COOLER

2 **lemon wedges**

1 **lime wedges**

1 **orange wedges**

5 **tangerine segments**, peeled

1 ounce **simple syrup** (see page 7)

1 ounce ruby red **grapefruit juice**

Splash of **soda water**

In a cocktail shaker, muddle the lemon, lime, and orange wedges with the tangerine segments and simple syrup. Add the grapefruit juice. Top with ice and shake vigorously. Pour into a tall glass. Top with the soda water.

101

Watermelon-Grape CRUSH

¼ cup fresh **watermelon chunks**

10 seedless **red grapes**

2 **basil leaves** (optional)

1½ ounces fresh **lime juice**

1½ ounces **simple syrup** (see page 7)

Splash of **soda water** (or **7-Up** for a sweeter drink)

In a cocktail shaker, muddle the watermelon with the grapes and leaves. Add the lime juice and simple syrup. Top with ice and shake vigorously. Strain into a tall glass and top with the soda water.

Index